GW00703353

Other books by Exley:
Teddy Bear Quotations
Cat Quotations
Cat Lover's Notebook
Cats a Celebration
Teddy Bears a Celebration

Published simultaneously in 1993 by Exley Publications in Great Britain, and Exley Giftbooks in the USA.
Second edition 1994.
Reprinted 1995.

EDITED BY HELEN EXLEY
Border illustrations by Bridgit Flinn

ISBN 1-85015-427-9

A copy of the CIP data is available from the British Library on request.

Pictures and quotations selected by Helen Exley.
Designed by Pinpoint Design.
Picture research by P. A. Goldberg and J. Clift/Image Select, London.
Typeset by Delta, Watford.
Printed and bound by Grafo, S.A., Bilbao, Spain.

Exley Publications Ltd, 16 Chalk Hill, Watford, Herts WDl 4BN, United Kingdom.
Exley Giftbooks, 232 Madison Avenue, Suite 1206, New York, NY 10016, USA.
Picture credits: Fine Art Photographic Library: cover; Maria Teresa Meloni: title page; Alison Trask, through Montague Ward, Wadhurst: pages 8, 27, 42, 49; Ann Stutt, through Montague Ward, Wadhurst: page 46; Bridgeman Art Library, London: page 36; Bridgit Flinn: page 31; Fine Art Photographic Library: pages 14, 28; John Clayton: pages 6, 17, 34, 50, 56, 60; Penny Gerken, through Montague Ward, Wadhurst: page 55; Phyllis Nelson: pages 44, 53; Popperfoto: pages 20, 24, 39, 59; Wendy Trinder, through Montague Ward; Wadhurst: pages 13, 22, 32.

TEDDY
• *Lovers* •
ADDRESS BOOK

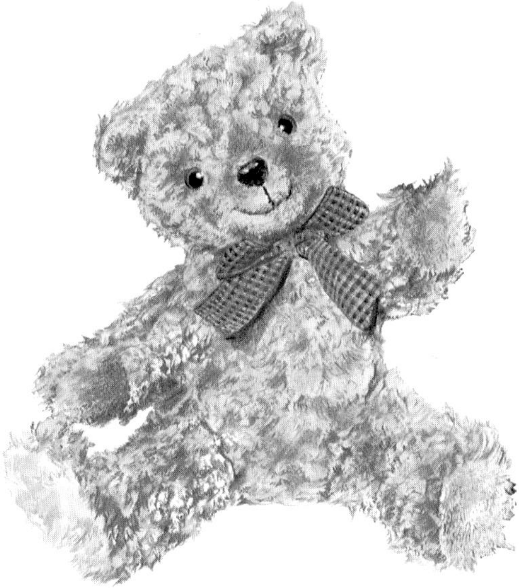

EDITED BY HELEN EXLEY

EXLEY
NEW YORK • WATFORD, UK

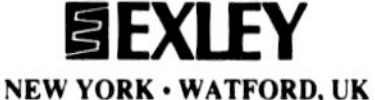

John Clayton

There's no bear like an old bear.

SAMANTHA ARMSTRONG

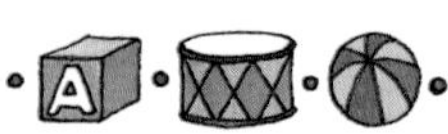

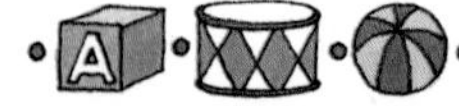

B

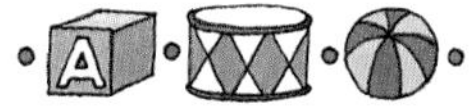

World Government Needs Bears.

HELEN EXLEY, B.1943

C

There probably isn't one among us who can't remember the comforting effect of cuddling up to a teddy bear at night.

RACHEL NEWMAN, FROM "COUNTRY BEARS"

C

John Clayton

C

Bears are just about the only toy that can lose just about everything and still maintain their dignity and worth.

SAMANTHA ARMSTRONG

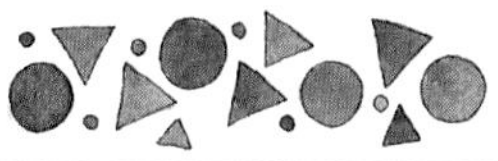

ETHEL PARKINSON.

G

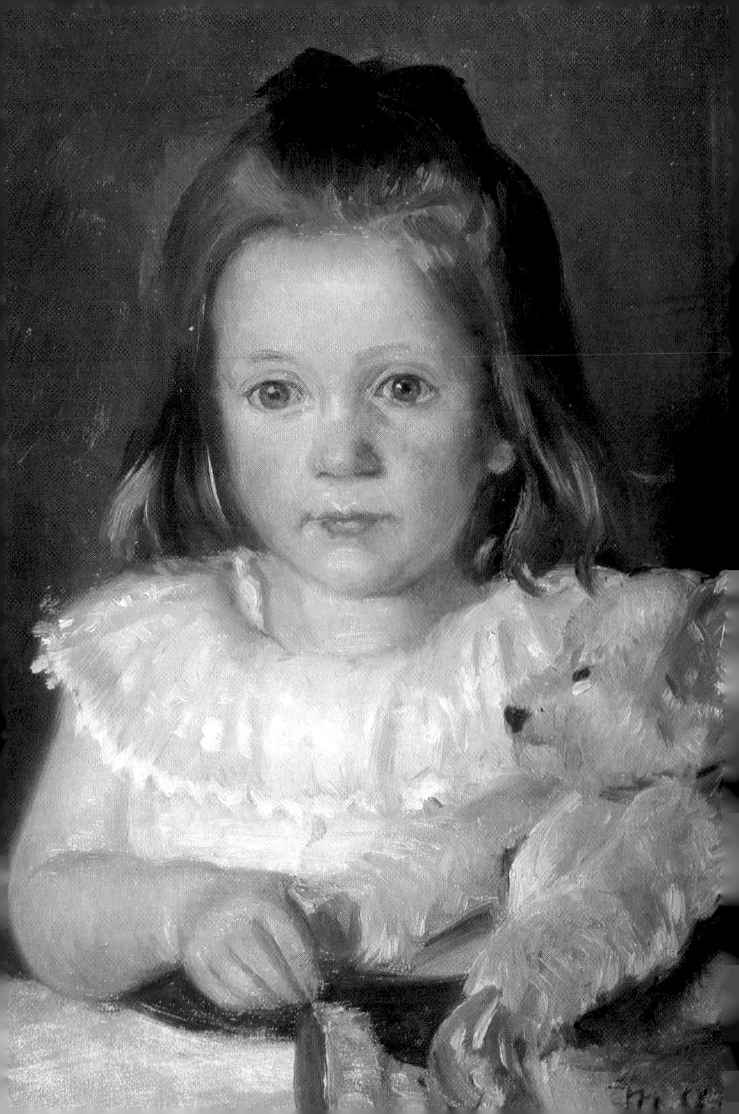

H

All you have between you and "The Dark" is Bear.

HELEN THOMSON

The basic ingredient in any leaving-home case is the bear.

JOHNNIE HAGUE

John Clayton

K

L

You need a bear to get you through measles. Especially when you're supposed to have grown up.

CLARA ORTEGA

1
2
4

M

A bear is as alive as you need him to be.

PETER GRAY

M

A bear grows more alive with age. No one with one ounce of sensitivity could ever consign a bear to the dustbin.

JOHNNIE HAGUE

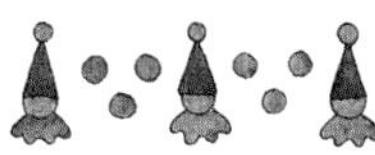

P/Q

The world is divided into two nations. Those with teddy bears, those without. Each thinks the other odd.

JENNY DE VRIES

John Clayton

S

S

It takes a lot of loving to turn a shop bear into a friend.

PAM BROWN, B.1928

S

Now that I'm all grown up, I can buy any old Teddy Bear I want – except the old Teddy Bear I want.

WILLIAM STERNMAN

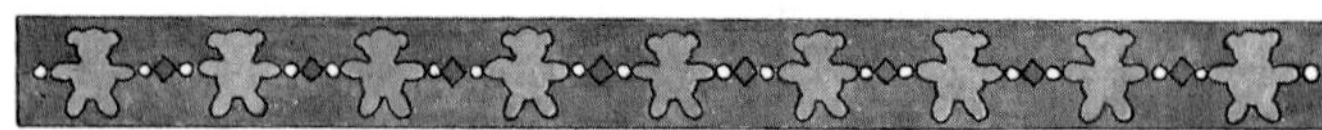

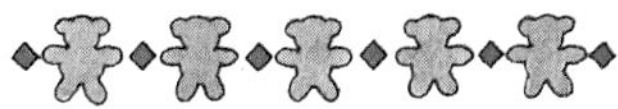

John Clayton

X/Y/Z

When everyone else has let you down, there's always Ted.

CLARA ORTEGA